LEARNING, LEAVENING, AND LEVITY

HOW BLACK LEADERS THRIVE IN UNCERTAIN TIMES

HARRY H. HAWKINS, III

HUMAN CAPITAL CONVERSIONS, LLC

CONTENTS

Introduction

This book was born when I was asked a simple yet profound question: "Is there a reference for all the concepts you've discussed?"

The question came from a leader who appreciated some of the tools and tips I shared as the lead faculty for Justified Anger's Leadership Institute. Unfortunately, I had to admit that there wasn't a single book or reference that compiled all the information and knowledge I offered to the leaders enrolled in the course.

I decided to create a reference where a Black leader could learn, review, and master all the tools and concepts I presented in the training sessions.

Here it is!

I bring thirty years of leadership experience to bear as I write these words. I have associate and bachelor's degrees in business administration and a master's degree in transformational leadership. I'm currently in my third year as a Ph.D. student on the Innovative Leadership Development track.

As a Black leader, I have experienced being dismissed, overly scru-tinized, falsely accused, demoted, fired, and rejected. But more than that, I've been mentored, trained, developed, promoted, trusted, and seen by many of my bosses and mentors over the years. For that invest-ment, I owe a debt of gratitude, and this book is the first installment of my repayment.

I write for a Black audience, with the Black leader in mind. Anyone can benefit from the concepts and tools, but understand, before you venture into this work, that I wrote it for Black leaders. If you aren't Black, you'll most likely need to translate the work into your cultural and social context. Consider it a bonus cross-cultural experiment for those who need it.

You're welcome!

I hope this book is easy to read, fun to engage with, and a reference that can be the starting point for mastering your leadership journey and bringing positive change to the world.

Even as social realities and political climates shift, the work doesn't stop; it simply evolves!

How to Read This Book

This book is divided into three sections.

The first describes the change management process that can be applied in any social or political context, but is especially useful during times of resistance to change or backlash from change. Odd-numbered chapters academically explain a topic or concept. Every academic chapter begins with a key thought to make it easier to understand the theme of the chapter. The even-numbered chapters add a little humor to the process, connected to the theme of the preceding chapter.

If you want to skip the humor, read the odd chapters.

If you're having a hard day, read the even chapters and laugh at my life and some of my bad choices!

The next section is a leadership toolbox, where I describe many of the practices I've used to put the principles from the first section into action. Each tool is labeled and designed to be a quick read. The explanations are not exhaustive, but they introduce meaningful concepts. I suspect that many of the tools I mention are already familiar to you, but perhaps you've never articulated them. Either way, I trust you'll be able to make good use of the tools when you see them.

The third section is a list of books that have shaped my ideas and character. Pick from this list as you see fit. Don't feel pressured to read all of them. It is a small sample, a few of my favorites that I've read over the years while pursuing multiple degrees. At the time of writing, I'm working on my fourth, a Ph.D. in Innovative Urban Leadership. So again, don't feel pressured to make your way through the entire list. It's there to serve you, not overwhelm you under a cascade of paper.

All that to say, read and approach this book in whatever way is helpful. If even one part helps you become a transformational leader, then it was worth my time to write it.

May my insights and quirks serve you well!

CHAPTER 1: LEAVENING

> **Key thought:** Even small, simple organisms like yeast can have a tremendous impact on their surroundings. Black leaders need a framework that allows them to influence their surroundings in all seasons. But we also need laughter as a salve for the soul-taxing work of existing in society.

What is leavening? And why did I start the book this way? Webster's defines leaven as "to mingle or permeate with some modifying, alleviating, or vivifying element" (Merriam-Webster.com Dictionary, n.d.). Yeast is a leavening agent when added to flour to make bread rise.

But that doesn't fully answer the question: *why*? When change is happening and it's popular to advocate for Black rights, or for equality, or for any other issues facing Black people today, action steps are easy. Your place in the struggle is clearly defined. Are you organizing the rally or meeting with executives to talk about policy changes? Are you applying for a new grant, updating your organization's website, or leading an affinity group at your workplace?

But what happens when the change you're hoping for is no longer desired or accepted? What do you do as a Black leader when your efforts to claim basic rights mark you as a problem employee or unfit for leadership roles?

In times like these, a different style of leadership is needed. In fact, I would argue that even in times when change is rolling forward, the lessons in this book can be used regardless of the season you find yourself in.

The process I use is called cultural leavening. Like yeast, you are an agent of change that, though small, can have a profound impact on your environment.

Yeast, a single-celled fungus, is present all around us. For yeast to work, however, it needs four elements: the right temperature, fuel, proximity, and time (Miller, 2020). For cultural leavening, you will need these four elements as well: atmosphere, fuel, proximity, and time. Throughout the book, I will dive deeper into these categories and lay out a series of skills and actions you can use that will withstand the test of time, politics, and budget cuts.

I will also add levity, "excessive or unseemly frivolity" (Merriam-Webster.com Dictionary, 2025a), throughout the book as an equal partner in underground resistance and social change. You will need both, and I hope to offer you a mix of the two that is at times explanatory and enjoyable.

So, let's jump right in!

Chapter 2: Use a Recipe

Years ago, as a bachelor (this detail is important only so no one blames my wife or my mother for the following fiasco), I decided I wanted biscuits for breakfast. But I was out of my mix. No problem, I thought I'll just make the biscuits from scratch. I had flour, after all, and how hard could it be?

If you cook at all, you probably know this is where I went wrong.

Despite the fact that I had multiple computers, all with internet access, I didn't bother looking up a recipe. Instead, I tried to create biscuits from memory. The problem with this approach was simple: I had never made biscuits from scratch on my own. Ever. So there was no memory to call on.

I dumped some flour in a bowl, added water, a little salt, and, I'm not even sure what else. It was white like dough, but thick. Really thick. Easy enough to fix, I thought. Just add more water until the dough had the "right" consistency. I floured the counter, rolled the dough out, cut the biscuits, popped them on a pan, and put them in the oven.

When the timer went off, I checked my creation. Sure enough, I had made some sort of bread product that resembled a biscuit, but didn't look quite right. Undeterred, I grabbed one, placed it on my plate, cut it open, and plopped a healthy spoonful of jelly on top.

Something happened that drew me away from my plate, but when I returned, the glob of jelly was gone. All that remained was a purple stain where the jelly had been. Most people would have stopped right there. Not me. I just added more jelly and kept going.

When I finally sat down to eat the biscuit, the first bite changed my mind. The round white disc I affectionately called "biscuit" was nothing short of the bread version of a black hole. Like the jelly before me, it sucked all the moisture straight out of my mouth. I could barely chew. I did not finish it. I could not. I needed to rehydrate before I could eat anything else.

Now, I use recipes if I have not made a dish before. In the same way, if you have not ushered in social change or learned how to lead as a Black leader in turbulent times, please do not just throw some stuff together and call it progress. Let us be precise and professional in our pursuit of liberty and justice for all.

CHAPTER 3: ATMOSPHERE

> **Key thought:** Yeast is common in the atmosphere, but for it to affect the environment, it needs the right temperature and water. Black leaders are the same. To thrive, we need the right environment to flourish.

Let me start with some sobering facts. Many Americans report being unhappy, especially those under 60 (Aubrey, 2024; Gallup Inc., 2024). Most U.S. employees report being disengaged at work (Marciano, 2010). Nearly 70 percent of all change initiatives fail (Pascale et al., 2000). On top of that, innovations are often resisted or rejected when they are introduced (Vincent, 2017).

One of the most critical skills a leader can have is reckoning with the truth. Webster's defines reckon as "to settle accounts, to make a calculation, or to accept something as certain" (Merriam-Webster.com Dictionary, 2025b).

How can you survive what you do not understand? How can you change what you will not accept as fact? Illusions are expensive fantasies that rob you of efficacy and potency when you want to make an impact as a leader. Abandon them every chance you get.

Is your workplace somewhere you can grow and flourish? Is it a place where you can find the resources you need to survive and connect with others? In other words, can you articulate your needs in a workplace environment?

Accepting the truth must start from within. Regardless of the answer, you should have one. And if you cannot articulate those needs yet, or if the concept feels too vague, let us explore some key elements that I believe make up a healthy atmosphere. I will frame these elements as questions.

Why?

Because self-discovery drives out self-delusion!

Are you understood at work?

I hold no illusions that you can bring your full self to work if you are Black. And please, do not be Black, talented, and educated. I am not referring to an ideal job where you are free to be your whole self and everyone just seems to understand you. But are there parts of you that are safe to share at work, that others understand? Do you find mutual agreement with someone, or with a group of people, on professional topics at work?

I have worked a lot of jobs over the years: construction, telemarketing, library services, multiple customer service jobs, retail clothing sales, retail jewelry sales, management, security, armored truck services, insurance, grocery store restocking, and nonprofit leadership. I have been cussed out, had the police called on me in my own store, been blamed for someone else's poor decisions, chastised for following the rules, and had my ideas stolen by a supervisor.

What made the difference between a good experience and a nightmare was how connected I was to others at the job. The places where I was understood, even a little, made all the difference.

At one job, that understanding came in the form of Ms. Pat, my boss, who recognized my desperate need for work of any kind. I was recently married and unemployed. She saw my résumé and knew I wanted to go back to school. During the interview, she voiced concern that I might leave after a few months once I was back in school. I explained my situation, and she believed me.

Another example was James, who hired me and recognized that I needed professional guidance. He gave me a system to work with and allowed me to navigate a profession I had assumed I was ill-suited for: sales.

Dianne, another influential boss, once asked me about my extra-long lunches. At the time, I was going through a divorce and needed to pick up my kids from school to drop them off at the babysitter's. She worked out a special arrangement for me.

I could list many more examples. The point is, whenever I found someone, especially a supervisor, who understood something about me and valued who I was, it had an enormous impact on my ability to thrive in that workplace.

With Ms. Pat, the convenience store she managed was sold, and I stayed with her until the store transitioned. James Miller trained me to be his replacement at a small-box retailer, preparing me to manage the store after he stepped down. Dianne gave me an opportunity to grow in jewelry sales and helped me navigate a challenging personal season filled with doubt.

As a leader, however, the question must go beyond self-reflection. While you deserve to be understood if you are the leader or supervisor, you must also ask a follow-up question: do you understand the people you work with?

If you study facilitation as a discipline, the same advice appears again and again: you must first understand others before you can persuade them of anything (Linden, 2010). Embracing this one concept can transform your leadership and change the lives of those around you.

Years ago, when I managed a retail jewelry store, I scheduled an interview with a young woman who was moving to the city to attend school. The company I worked for was a subsidiary of a larger jewelry conglomerate, and as such, we shared a recruiting system with a sister chain.

A day or so before the interview, I received a call from the manager of one of the sister locations. He had interviewed the young woman before me, and something had happened during their meeting that led him to warn me against hiring her. He told me she was "crazy" and said I shouldn't even bother interviewing her.

I thanked him for the heads-up and decided to interview her anyway. I prefer to make up my own mind about who I interview and hire, and I was curious. When she arrived, she interviewed well, even though she had no prior jewelry experience. As part of my usual process for sales candidates, I asked her to do a role-play demonstration. She impressed me with two things. First, she shared some information about pearls that I didn't know, which was surprising since I was one of the few people in the company with training and certification in gemstones, including pearls. Second, she displayed a genuine passion for jewelry.

I hired her and trained her in sales, but she brought a flair and dedication that were uniquely her own. Thirteen years later, she opened her own jewelry store and credits her success to the opportunity I gave her to enter the jewelry business.

I had recognized her transferable skills and her passion for serving people. She turned that combination into a career and, ultimately, into her calling.

Can you influence others?

Innovators know that to create new ideas and processes, you need to be close to the people who are using the idea, process, or product (Kelley, 2001). If you are a Black leader, then you must be close enough to the people who are change makers in your organization to bring innovation and see change through successfully.

At the beginning of this chapter, I told you that most change initiatives fail (Pascale et al., 2000). While there are many causes for this high rate of failure, one truth emerges: you cannot change what you cannot touch. Innovators call it being close to the action (Kelley, 2001, p. 31). Theologians recognize the need to shape culture from the inside (Hunter, 2010, p. 8).

One obvious challenge is that to influence others, you must first earn their trust. To be trusted, you need credibility (Linden, 2010).

Let me explain with an example. A co-worker comes in on Monday raving about a movie they saw over the weekend. They tell you to see it immediately. Do you check it out? Do you ask questions? Your response probably depends on the person making the recommendation. Do they know what kind of movies you enjoy? Have they recommended films in the past that you liked? Do you share similar tastes?

Do you have enough relationship capital to make a suggestion and have someone follow your advice? If not, I recommend a simple way to start building it: allow yourself to be influenced by others. If you are low on relationship capital, do not have strong ties at work, and cannot yet make an impact, remember that people want to be understood. If you apply curiosity to their work, their life, or any area they are open to, you will find a place to begin.

Try the new restaurant someone mentioned. Try a new software application at work. Listen to a new song. Whatever it takes to start building a road of influence. I have found that people are far more interested in what I have to say once they see I am genuinely interested in them as people.

One of the best ways to build connections is by sharing new experiences with others. Influence is the vehicle that makes this possible. By modeling openness to being influenced yourself, you can foster a culture that values influence and embraces shared experiences.

Do not underestimate the power of sharing, even when it comes to small or seemingly insignificant parts of your life. A funny story, a new recipe, or even a hobby can open the door to deeper conversations and stronger relationships. Small connections often become stepping-stones to meaningful ones.

For the purpose of this chapter, those small connections at the very least create the kind of atmosphere that provides moments of respite and humanity in your workplace.

<u>Do you have a healthy work-life rhythm?</u>

Why didn't I say work-life balance? "Balance" implies some sort of equality. But if you work 8 of the 16 hours you are awake (assuming you get close to 8 hours of sleep), you already spend most of your waking hours at work. Balance also conjures the image of a scale, where the two items being measured are compared against one another and their weights are static. Real life is not static. You don't just have work, but also a spouse, children, pets, extended family, aging parents, friends, emergencies, grocery shopping, chores, healthcare appointments, and a host of other responsibilities that pull on your time.

That is why I use the phrase life rhythm. It invokes the image of a chorus of instruments playing their parts to an agreed tempo and style, coming together to make a beautiful song. That song can shift in tempo or style, add or drop instruments as needed. In short, it provides a framework that accepts and honors the flexibility life requires.

So, do you have a healthy work-life rhythm? Does work harmonize with the rest of your life, or does it add disharmony to the symphony of your week?

Do you find yourself working after hours on a regular basis? Do you give up your days off to finish projects or change personal plans frequently? And if you do, is there acknowledgment of that sacrifice once the deadline is met or the goal is achieved?

This concept is easy to discuss but hard to define. Why? Because no one can tell you what the right mix of work and life is for you. I know people who love working second shifts because they hate getting up early. I know others who prefer weekends at work so they can enjoy weekdays for errands, quieter shopping, or doctor appointments.

The point is not about a perfect formula. The point is about whether your life has a rhythm that ebbs and flows together. Do you have that?

Chapter 4: Courtesy Wipe

"We need to talk." One of the most dreaded phrases you can hear in the workplace. And that's how this story starts. My supervisor walked up to me and dropped that line out of nowhere.

But let me give you a little background. I was working in a jewelry store, the only Black person there, and I was having a rough time fitting in. Some of that was on me. I was completely over working in retail and desperate for a way out. But some of it had to do with the job itself, especially the way customer distribution was handled.

You see, in most sales jobs I had worked before, there was a system of "ups" that determined who would greet and help the next customer. These systems kept people from being swarmed by overeager sales staff the moment they walked through the door. In my experience, it was always a simple, first-come, first-serve setup. But this company decided that every salesperson should get the same number of customers. More often than not, this meant that the person with the fewest sales ended up stuck at the desk during the slowest part of the day, when most people were at work.

On top of that, I was on a health journey, trying to figure out what I should eat and what I needed to avoid to keep my allergies under control. On this particular day, I had landed on eating a massive amount of collard greens.

So here is the situation: I am stuck at the front, greeting customers because it is my turn. As usual, business slowed down between 1 p.m. and 5 p.m. It was right after lunch, and I could not just walk away, because we all had to get the same number of sales. Meanwhile, thanks to those collard greens, a growing need to relieve some intestinal pressure was becoming harder and harder to ignore.

Well, one woman came in to have her ring cleaned. I took her ring to the polishing room, which was located next to the bathrooms. This room had no windows but did have a hood to vent the fumes that built up during the polishing process. As I was polishing and cleaning the ring, I started to get comfortable. You know that relaxed state you fall into when you are alone and need to be free. Well, I relaxed a little too much and released the fart I had been holding for a while.

I regretted that choice immediately. When the smell hit me, I knew I had made a bad life decision. I panicked. I turned on the hood, hoping it would suck away the stench, but it was not working fast enough. So, I opened the door and began "fanning" the air with it, hoping to spread the smell thin and break the curse of the greens. Once I was done, I grabbed the ring, left the polishing room, and returned to the customer.

I sat down, and honestly, I felt pretty good. Balance had been restored in my gut, and I felt a little lighter, like the sun was shining brighter. That is when my manager came over to me and uttered the dreaded words, "We need to talk."

I was shocked. His face was twisted, and he looked angry. I had struggled a few months earlier with my sales goal, but lately I had been doing well and thought everything was fine. Astonished, I asked what he wanted to talk about.

"Was that you?" he asked.

"What?"

"Was that you? Did you do that?" He pointed toward the polishing room.

You see, while I was helping my last customer, my co-workers were assisting others who also needed their rings polished. When they walked past the polishing room, they caught the scent of my shame lingering in the hallway. At first, they thought it was coming from the bathrooms. But when they stepped into the polishing room, their noses were assaulted by the angry smoke creature I had left behind.

My supervisor went on to tell me how disgusted he was as we all laughed, though not everyone found it funny. I apologized and explained my mistake, blaming it on my overconsumption of collard greens. For the rest of the night, my co-workers teased and joked with me about it. Then my supervisor asked a question that made me laugh so hard I cried.

"Did you at least do a courtesy wipe? Just to make sure?"

I had never heard of such a thing, and that, combined with the relentless joking from the men (the women were not amused), made it a memorable day.

For me, while I struggled at times being the only Black person in the store, moments like this helped me connect with both the people and the culture of the workplace. The openness of my supervisor and his willingness to address even awkward situations made it easier to work there.

Chapter 5: Fuel for Change

Key thought: Yeast used for cooking is often in a dormant state. To make it useful, the yeast needs the right temperature and water, which we can describe as the atmosphere. But atmosphere alone is not enough. The yeast also needs sugar, or it will not activate. Black leaders are similar. We need the right fuel at work to be engaged.

What do you need to be engaged at work? First, let us define what engagement means in a work context.

"Employee engagement is the emotional commitment the employee has to the organization and its goals" (Kruse, 2012).

In short, employees who are engaged are more productive, more loyal, and less likely to leave than disengaged employees (Marciano, 2010).

Dr. Paul Marciano (2010) highlights ten key traits of an engaged employee:

- Brings new ideas to work

- Is passionate and enthusiastic about work
- Takes initiative
- Actively seeks to improve self, others, and business
- Consistently exceeds goals and expectations
- Is curious and interested; asks questions
- Encourages and supports team members
- Is optimistic and positive; smiles
- Overcomes obstacles and stays focused on tasks; is persistent
- Is committed to the organization

Does this list describe you at work? If not, why not? What would you need in order to feel more engaged with your work?

Research has uncovered three themes that contribute to employee engagement. The first is having a good relationship with your supervisor, one built on respect and trust (Marciano, 2010). The second is the opportunity to contribute to something greater than yourself. The third is the need to be recognized as competent in your work (Linden, 2010).

Relationship with your Boss

Above all else, this is the number one factor that can either create an engaged employee or drive someone to quit. How people interact with and report to their supervisor is the most crucial element of building engagement.

So, how is your relationship with your boss? Do you respect them as both a professional and a person? Do they respect you and your contributions to the workplace? Have you received praise in the last two weeks for your performance? If you have a question or run into a problem, do you feel comfortable going to your manager to discuss it?

This element is difficult to control, since your relationship with your manager is not entirely in your hands. Still, here is my advice on how to do your part to foster a positive relationship with your boss.

First, do you understand what they need and want from work? Are they hoping for a promotion? Are they focused on their bonus? Are they simply trying to retire without incident or controversy? Whatever motivates them to succeed, you need to become an expert in supporting that goal, or at least helping them meet that need when possible.

I must add a word of caution, however. Following this approach can sometimes backfire. At times in my career, when I adopted this attitude and delivered, my boss became suspicious of my motives. They could see my talent and became intimidated by my ability to perform. Some even began to fear that I might take their job.

In those cases, I had to either pull away and try to "keep my head down" or decide to move on to another job. Sometimes I was promoted while they were demoted. Other times I was fired or "harassed" and suddenly could not do anything right in my supervisor's eyes. If you are Black and talented, this is a real challenge, and it requires finesse and professionalism to overcome. Later, we will discuss my triangle of protection, a tool that can give you leverage and security in situations where your excellence is viewed as a threat instead of an asset.

Either way, you need to gauge your relationship with your supervisor to see if it is one that can be uplifting or at least a stabilizing influence in your work life. If it is not, it becomes extremely difficult to thrive and remain engaged when you and your manager are not aligned.

Part of Something Larger than Yourself

The next element we need in order to truly thrive as leaders is a connection to something larger than ourselves. "Most people need to feel a sense of competence or mastery in some part of their lives and need to be part of something larger than themselves" (Linden, 2010, p. 22).

Are you connected emotionally to the mission of your company or organization? Do you get a genuine sense of satisfaction knowing you helped the team accomplish its goals?

First, we need to recognize that the organization has a responsibility to provide you with the resources and feedback needed to understand your impact on its goals. If you do not have that, begin by trying to discover your impact, even if no one else provides the data to you.

Once you have that, ask yourself: Do you care about what the company does? Or is it simply a job, something to get you through this stage of life?

I want to pause here to share a bit of encouragement. For most of my career, I would not have answered yes to that question. And that is okay. As a Black man, I did not always have the luxury of choosing a job I was passionate about. Sometimes I had to take work simply so my family could eat and have a roof over their heads. In those times, when I did not feel connected to the company's mission, my connections with my boss and my co-workers made all the difference. It was far easier to get excited about helping a friend at work accomplish a goal than about making sure a quarterly stockholder report showed growth.

If you are not emotionally connected to the larger mission, try substituting that connection with the journeys and lives of the people around you. The goal is to have something worth working for beyond selfish desires or even your family's needs.

In every case where I lacked a connection to the mission or the people, I became miserable at work, and the drudgery set in. Eventually, this drained my energy, and my work ethic suffered.

In short, my advice is that work should fulfill some purpose in your life, ideally. But what if it does not? What can you do then? I suggest spending some time learning about yourself. Why are you not connected to the company's mission? What about the environment makes it difficult to connect with others? If you were in charge, what changes would you make?

Once you have that list, try to influence the culture of the organization from your position. Have fun with it, but be respectful and stay within the structure of authority.

For example, let us say you started a job that offered no training. You managed to figure things out, but now you see a new hire struggling with the same challenges. Could you jot down a short bulleted list of tips you wish you had when you started? Do not spend more than fifteen minutes on the task, since it is extra, but it could be satisfying and may even reveal a passion for training you did not know you had.

The idea is to invest a small amount of effort so you can test multiple things along the way. Do not give too much, because that is a trap. I recommend offering only what you feel comfortable giving, and only if it takes just a few minutes to complete. If, once you are finished, you feel the need to be thanked, paid extra, or formally recognized, then you have gone too far and given too much. Think napkin notes rather than a 40-page PowerPoint presentation.

Seen as Competent

This idea leads us to the third element we need in order to be fueled and engaged at work: leaders must be seen as competent in their work. While this is true for all employees, Black leaders need it for many additional reasons. Maybe you had a bad experience in school, or people assumed you were unintelligent growing up. Maybe you were teased because you excelled in school. Maybe you have never been acknowledged as a leader at work or anywhere else. Or maybe you have had to prove yourself far beyond your peers simply because others did not recognize your value and worth.

Regardless of the reason, Black leaders must be seen as competent. If you are not recognized as competent at work, what should you do? First, I suggest becoming an expert in documentation. Why? If recognition is difficult to come by in your workplace, chances are that blame is easy to pick up. For this reason, you should document your processes, your ideas, and especially the challenges you face in completing tasks or collaborating with others.

For example, years ago I worked in a jewelry store where we held a weekly manager's meeting. I wanted to know what my section of the business was doing well and what needed improvement. Each week, I required my staff to fill out a short report, which I combined with other data to create a weekly summary that measured how effectively we were meeting our goals. During the meetings, I would present my report, explaining our areas of weakness, whether it was a team-wide issue or the result of a single person's performance, and outlining my plans to close those gaps.

One of my counterparts did not gather the same amount or quality of data. Each week, my ability to demonstrate our team's progress highlighted my competence and leadership. Eventually, I took her position and went on to earn a series of promotions in that job. I believe no one should know my work and its impact better than I do.

Asking questions to raise awareness is a companion skill to documentation. If you are working on a team or dealing with co-workers who do not carry their weight, the best way I have found to protect myself is by asking questions. Send an email asking for clarification. Outline your understanding of the project. Ask for a meeting to iron out difficult details or request a redirect if needed. Whatever the issue, try to resolve it on your own, and if that does not work, include your questions as part of your documentation process. The goal is to maintain a written record of what happened, what steps you took to correct the situation, and why you either succeeded or failed in meeting the goal.

One key point: do not overuse this strategy. You should not turn it into an annoyance by emailing about every little detail. If you are working with a long document or a series of detailed exchanges, consider attaching a file or linking to the full text. In your email or memo, keep the message brief and provide a summary. Always suggest a plan of action to resolve the issue. You want to make it as easy as possible for your supervisor to say yes without burdening them with extra work or lengthy reading.

In summary, you need to be engaged at work if you want to thrive. It is nearly impossible to do your best work if you are not emotionally present with what you are doing. And if you decide that your current workplace is not the best fit, before you leave, consider how you will answer the following interview question: "Why are you leaving your current employer?"

If you cannot answer this without speaking negatively about your employer, you need to pause and reflect on the true reasons for your decision. Sometimes we have bad days and become very emotional. That is fine, and it can be perfectly reasonable to leave an employer as a result. But if you have done the work to understand what you need in order to be engaged, you can explain why it is time for you to move on without disparaging your current workplace.

You can simply state which needs your current employer failed to meet and what steps you took to try to fill the gap. This reflection will also provide you with valuable questions to ask a potential employer during the interview process, helping you determine whether the new role can meet the needs that keep you engaged.

Chapter 6: Phone Call and a Prayer

For most of my career, I did not have the privilege of working in a field I truly desired or had expertise in. I had to find work wherever I could to provide for my family. Part of this was because of challenges surrounding the completion of my undergraduate education. In order to thrive in jobs I did not always love, I learned to make strong connections with my co-workers and to infuse humor into my day.

At one particular job, I was a jewelry manager, and during the fourth quarter we held our annual sales event. As part of the promotion, each salesperson had to call from a list of the store's customers and invite them to the event. I hated making those calls, truthfully, we all did. I preferred to get the task over with quickly, so I would try to call everyone on my list in one sitting. Depending on the size of the list, it could take one to two hours.

To make the process less painful, I would often call during rush hour, when people were less likely to answer because they were in transit. It was much easier to leave a message than to actually have a conversation.

On this particular night, I stepped away from the sales floor and began making my calls. The script went something like this:

"Hello, this message is for John Doe. This is Harry from the Famous Jewelry Store, and I wanted to invite you to our annual sales extravaganza. We've mailed you a rewards card and a 15 percent off coupon, so keep an eye out for that. We hope to see you soon! Take care and good night!"

I had repeated the script so many times that I could say it without thinking. But as it turned out, sitting for two hours making mindless calls around 5 p.m. was the perfect recipe for falling asleep. And that is exactly what happened. I began dozing off while making my calls. The crazy part is that I somehow kept talking, even as I dipped in and out of consciousness. I should have stopped, stretched, or taken a quick walk around. But no, I wanted to finish as quickly as possible.

So, on one call, I started falling asleep as I was talking, and I guess my mind thought I was at home in bed. My brain must have interpreted my actions as bedtime prayer. As I finished my rehearsed and memorized speech, I ended the call with, "In Jesus' name, Amen!"

That snapped me awake. I pulled the phone away from my face and looked at it, then looked around. I stared at the phone base, wondering how I could take back that last sentence. Unfortunately, there was no way I knew of to erase the message, so I just hung up.

That was the end of my calls for the night. I sat there processing what I had just done and what consequences might come from my impromptu prayer. I worried that my sleepy blessing might turn into an employment curse, but eventually I shrugged and let it go. After all, what could I do about it?

Soon, it became funny to me. As I shook off my mid-shift nap, I started telling my co-workers what had happened. They all thought it was hilarious, and we laughed and laughed. Later that evening, our District Manager came into the store, and I figured he would appreciate a good bit of humor as well.

He did not. In fact, he seemed rather disturbed by my unintended benediction.

If you are not thriving at work and cannot leave right away, find something that gives you a reason to show up beyond a paycheck. But if you happen to slip in a prayer or two, take my advice: do not tell your manager.

Chapter 7: Proximate to the Action

> **Key Thought:** Yeast must be kneaded into the dough for it to do its work. Black leaders must be connected to the action in order to know where and how to change the environment and activate others.

The next step in bringing change as a leader is to be close to the action. Who makes the decisions in your organization? How are decisions made? Who influences the boss? Who slows down progress or blocks change? To truly understand how to create impact, you must understand organizational culture.

Organizational culture is not a vision statement. It is not a mission statement. Webster's defines culture as "the set of shared attitudes, values, goals, and practices that characterizes an institution or organization" (Definition of *Culture*, 2025).

Culture cannot be reduced to a single phrase. It is complex, with deep roots in both self-identity and group identity. Ethnicity, age, gender, religion, regional influences, and many other factors shape people, and people in turn create, support, enforce, and influence the collective culture of any organization.

So how can you identify the culture in your organization?

Permanent Culture

I will use two terms to help you identify culture. The first is *permanent culture*. This refers to the parts of culture that typically do not change, or if they do, it takes a great deal of time and effort.

Think of it like making chicken noodle soup. The base is a broth of chicken stock. You must add chicken and noodles. These ingredients are what give the soup its name. If you change any of them, you are no longer making chicken noodle soup. It might still be soup, but its very nature will be different. For example, if you decide to make a soup with a cream base and then add chicken and noodles, you have created a completely different soup.

The same is true for any organization. There are elements of its culture that are core to its very existence. This is what I call permanent culture. These pieces will not change easily, no matter who works for the organization. Permanent culture is the sum of the attitudes, values, and practices upon which the organization stands. These elements form the foundation of the organization's very identity.

You can begin to understand the permanent culture of an organization by examining its legal classification. Is it a nonprofit, a government agency, or a for-profit retailer? Each classification usually carries legal requirements and restrictions that shape many of the practices, policies, and traditions of the group.

Are employees required to participate in an annual fundraiser? Does leadership shift after an election cycle? Are certain holidays off-limits for vacations? Many people move between different organizations throughout their careers, but rarely do they switch industries.

That is why identifying these foundational realities is essential. They may seem fixed or obvious, but they are part of the culture.

Another major contributor to culture is the set of industry and organizational standards that shape how people are hired, fired, and promoted, along with the overall purpose of the organization. Does your organization reward advanced degrees? Is tenure or seniority important? Or is it more of a meritocracy? Whatever the traditions, values, and practices may be, they all contribute significantly to organizational culture.

These elements often form the foundation of the permanent culture. For example, if you work for a retailer, evening and weekend shifts will likely be part of your schedule. If you work for a nonprofit, fundraising and grants may be central to your work. If you work for a religious institution, faith will inevitably be a part of your professional life. Permanent culture establishes the boundaries of what is permitted and what is considered taboo in the workplace.

Another monumental influence on organizational culture is the culture of the region where the business is located. For instance, when I moved to Madison from Atlanta, I was surprised to learn that gas stations did not stay open all night. On my first trip, I found myself searching for fuel in the early morning hours as I headed to the airport at 4:30 a.m. I was also surprised to see pumps that were not pre-pay and gas stations that still accepted checks. The smaller-town culture created a different reality for how gas stations operated.

Another example is the widely accepted practice of "buying local." In Atlanta, large chains were often viewed as stable and offering great value. In Madison, however, those same chains were seen as invaders, less connected to the community than locally owned independent stores.

Regional, cultural, and ethnic influences all strongly shape organizational culture, though they can be difficult to identify if you are deeply immersed in them. As a Black leader, you may easily spot the differences, but do you also understand why those differences exist?

Impermanent Culture

The next elements that make up impermanent culture are tied more closely to the people who work for the organization and the habits they bring with them. What type of food is eaten at the office? How do people view timeliness? Is the dress code a strict rule or simply a guideline? Impermanent culture often exists within the boundaries of permanent culture and can be difficult to distinguish if the group is homogenous, or nearly so.

This is one of the challenges in creating a diverse organization when you are starting with a homogenous group. It can be very difficult to separate impermanent culture from permanent culture. Let me illustrate.

One place where we often see this challenge is in marriage. Take a couple, the Williamses. Both come from families where meals were eaten together. When they married, they assumed that since they shared this cultural practice of family meals, everything would align. But in the husband's family, meals were eaten in front of the television, while in the wife's family, meals were shared at the dining table without TV. The tradition of eating together was part of their permanent culture, but the location and manner of eating were aspects of impermanent culture that differed.

After discussion, they might agree to eat at the table most days. On special occasions, when a favorite team was playing or a special show aired, they would eat in front of the television. In this way, they honored the permanent tradition of eating together while adjusting the impermanent culture to fit the needs of their new family.

In organizations, when diverse people are hired, the dynamic is less like a marriage and more like an adoption. The employee is not seen as an equal partner but as a new member of an established unit who must assimilate.

If you are attempting to diversify, I recommend involving someone from outside the organization who is not part of the dominant culture to help identify which aspects of the culture are permanent and which are impermanent. Do not place that burden on someone who belongs to the dominant culture, and never assign that responsibility to a diverse staff member.

If you were hired or promoted into a Director of Diversity position, or something similar, with the expectation that you would identify these issues and then change them, here is my advice: take a day off, use my F-it method (a tool in the leadership toolbox), and go hug a puppy. You are probably tired and exhausted. You have already identified the culture at work, and chances are you will roll your eyes when a consultant comes in and says exactly what you have been saying all along. Work with the consultant, but do not assume responsibility for challenging the established order and culture of the organization.

Here is why I say this. Although you may easily see the difference between permanent culture and impermanent culture, any changes you suggest could be viewed as an attack on the culture as a whole. Without clarifying the impermanent aspects of the company's culture, people often mistake surgery for execution. A small change may feel as if it is intended to transform the entire culture or way of life.

Secondly, one person cannot change a system. That may sound obvious, but I cannot tell you how many times I have spoken with Diversity and Inclusion Managers at mid- to large-sized firms who are either the only person working in Diversity or who do not have a real team at all. If a Diversity Manager does not have a team to manage, what are they really managing? Most likely, just the organization's public relations efforts.

Tension and Unrealized Goals

Once you start mapping out your organization's culture, the next step is to identify places of leverage. The easiest places for a leader to exert leverage are where there is organizational tension or where goals remain unmet. What do I mean?

Imagine this: your boss wants a promotion and has been very vocal about that desire. To earn it, your store needs to exceed its sales goal. You have a process you use every day that makes you successful. If you can show your boss how to train others to adopt your technique, the team might reach the sales goal and help your boss qualify for the promotion.

Here is another example. Two co-workers are not getting along. You understand the root of the problem, but neither of them will acknowledge the validity of the other's claims, even in part. By getting close to the action, you can listen to both sides, articulate their positions clearly, and ask thoughtful questions to help them navigate their differences. Either way, you position yourself as a trusted and reasonable voice.

Wherever you find people, you will find some form of social tension. If you can pluck that string, you may uncover a pathway to influence and effective leadership.

CHAPTER 8: KNUCKLE DIPPERS AND THE FLU

Years ago, I was asked to help with the communion service at my local church. I was a lay minister at the time, and my duties were simple: hold the cup and allow people to dip their communion bread into the juice. As it happened, this was in the fall, right around the time the flu tends to spread across the community.

People were called by section to get in line, and one by one, they dipped their bread into the cup. Most people just touched the tip of their bread into the juice and moved on. Some, however, perhaps struggling with hand-eye coordination, or maybe just wanting their bread fully baptized in the juice, dunked the entire piece. I would watch in horror as people went knuckle-deep into the juice, leaving behind a ring of oil that radiated out from where they broke the surface. It was like watching a tiny, terrified octopus release ink to escape predators, again and again. I even found myself trying to predict who might be a "knuckle dipper" as they approached. Totally the wrong mindset for the occasion.

As each person dipped, I could not imagine putting my own bread into that oil-slicked juice and then eating it. I'm a married man, I can't be that close to people!

Anyway, the servers usually participated in communion after the congregation was finished. As I waited for the line to die down, I looked around and thought, "Nope!" I was not taking communion that day. My internal dialogue was so amusing that I began to chuckle. Just a little at first. But then I pictured myself standing at the front of the church with this ridiculous half-smirk, half-grin on my face, and that made it even funnier.

What were people thinking? Did they wonder why I was laughing? Thankfully, I managed to pull myself together, realizing someone might think I was laughing at them. The last thing I wanted was to traumatize someone at church, so I reined it in.

Later, I shared my experience with other church leaders. I told them I was too nervous to participate after witnessing the "knuckle dippers" during communion. Once they finished laughing at my description, the leaders decided to switch to individually sealed communion cups.

Don't get me wrong, I enjoy extending the hand of fellowship at church. I just do not want to taste someone else's fingers on my communion bread.

Gross.

I think I just made myself sick writing this.

Chapter 9: Time

> **Key Thought:** One of the most amazing things about yeast is how much of a difference it makes in dough when it has everything it needs and a little time. Black leaders are the same. In the right environment, time becomes a blessing that can help a leader transform an organization from the inside.

At the time of writing this book, the United States is in a period where diversity initiatives are under attack. Some critics have gone so far as to call them illegal or examples of reverse discrimination. Just a few years ago, corporations were pledging their commitment to diversity, equity, and inclusion. Now many of those same corporations have publicly reversed their claims, while others have gone silent, quietly removing those promises from websites and handbooks.

This can be discouraging for those who hope for change. It can feel crushing to work toward a better world and workplace only to see that work dismantled so efficiently. Yet, as disturbing and demoralizing as it is, the truth remains: after successful advances in social justice, there is always pushback. For more on this, see the references section. I will not attempt a full scholarly treatment of the subject here, but chances are if you are Black and reading this, you already know it to be true.

So what is a Black leader to do?

Recognize that all change has a rhythm. Your job is to recognize the moment you are in and respond accordingly. If the winds of change are shifting in your favor and the ideals you promote are popular, or if people are receptive to ideas that disrupt their social equilibrium, then direct methods of protest and advocacy may be the right path. March and sign petitions. Write articles. Demand change from officials and public servants.

But when the moment shifts, do not worry. Simply pivot.

How? Let us begin by exploring the foundational reasons why changing unjust systems is necessary.

Years ago, I was the General Manager of a jewelry store and responsible for hiring. The company required us to use a standardized hiring process, complete with a pre-interview questionnaire, prescribed interview questions, and a payment calculator.

I conducted interviews using the system, never straying from the prescribed formula. During one interview with a new hire, I discovered that he played video games. I was pleasantly surprised, since I was a gamer myself. We talked briefly about games, and I thought little of it.

The very next person I hired turned out to be a gamer as well. I was surprised again. What a coincidence, two gamers in the building where, before I arrived, there had not been a single person who shared my love of the hobby.

Then it happened again with my next hire. I had followed the protocols to the letter. I never asked about hobbies, nor did they ask about mine. Yet somehow I had selected three gamers out of all the candidates who interviewed with me. The first time had been a surprise. The second felt like a coincidence. But three? Three was a pattern that was hard to ignore.

Before long, we had a building full of gamers, and I could not have been happier. I finally had people to discuss games with, and we even started playing mobile games together. While that was fun, it created some problems. Other staff began to sense that if you were not a gamer, I did not like you as much. I spent more time engaging with the "gamer staff" than with the others. That was an issue, but a relatively small one compared to the bigger problem. My success rate in hiring "good candidates" hovered around fifty percent. Half of the new hires were not the best fit for the job, despite the connection I felt with them during interviews.

So what went wrong? I had followed the company's protocols. I had obeyed the law. Yet in practice, my hiring decisions were no better than a coin toss.

The answer is that my unconscious bias picked up on the fact that I shared similarities with certain candidates. When it came down to choosing between two or three equally qualified applicants, I had to make a subjective choice. Which one was the right fit? Left to my own devices, the unconscious answer was usually the person most like me.

In situations like this, while I was legally avoiding discriminatory behavior, I was in fact finding ways to ascribe positive attributes to people who were similar to me. That led to higher turnover and disengaged employees because of the favoritism I showed.

During times of social or organizational change, an employee might call out behavior like this and demand some form of correction. That could mean implementing a hiring panel, changing the questions that are asked, or bringing in multiple interviewers. There are many options that can be used to minimize unintentional discrimination and its effects on workplace culture.

But what about those times when addressing social issues is not popular? My advice is to go to the root cause and connect the action to the negative outcomes for the manager and the company. In this case, the hiring process I followed contributed to higher turnover, disengaged employees, and a loss of productivity.

No matter the political climate or the presence or absence of social change agents, it is always the right time for a company to address issues of profit and productivity.

As a Black leader, you must choose your battles and your words carefully. If people are receptive to a concept like unconscious bias, then address it directly. If they are not, focus on the problems that result from it.

Diversity initiatives that do not address the root issues usually just pass the discrimination to another group. But if what you are working toward addresses the real issues, either approach can lead to the same result. I do not care if you order twelve donuts or a dozen donuts. If we cannot focus on diversity directly, then we can focus on reducing turnover and improving employee engagement. In many cases, the root cause is the same. I have found that organizations that discriminate against employees or build biases into their hiring processes also suffer from inefficiencies within the organization.

How do I know that? Imagine this: you are a hiring manager who hires based on the color of someone's shirt. If it matches the color you are wearing during the interview, then they are hired. Sure, you might stumble upon some great employees that way, but you will also hire a few poor fits. Some may not have the training they need. Others may lack the interpersonal skills necessary to work with others. Either way, you will face the need for extra training, handle more employee complaints, and spend too much time managing the blunders of incompetent hires and the disengagement of competent staff. When biases go unchecked, we inevitably hire problems. This is why timing is crucial in dealing with change.

Understanding timing is a key to mastering life. It can make the difference between a yes and a no. It can make the difference between inspiring someone toward greatness or crushing their confidence.

So how do you master time if you struggle with it in your own life? There are a few questions you can ask yourself to begin taking advantage of the power of timing:

What motivates this person?

What slows them down or gets them off track?

Do I see a repeating pattern?

What questions keep coming up?

When are they most receptive?

Essentially, I am describing a process where you can begin to understand what makes a person tick. What motivates them as employees? How do they process information?

For example, I do not want to talk to people before I eat my breakfast. Before 8:30, the answer to almost any question is likely to be "no." I am much friendlier and more relaxed after lunch. "Monday Harry" is better equipped to listen than "Friday Harry." A short email asking for permission to solve a problem, written with bullet points, will get a faster response than a long, detailed email that simply explains the problem.

If you know these things about me, you can steer me onto the path you want. Present me with a proposed solution in bullet points after lunch, and boom, you have a yes and a figurative pat on the back (gotta keep it HR-friendly)! But send me a long email at 7 a.m. and just drop the problem on my lap, and I will probably set it aside for later.

Timing is key.

Mastering time is not about perfection or always being on time. It is about navigating the space between people that often keeps us from understanding one another. All social change starts with personal transformation. Time, then, is your strongest ally in that fight. Use it wisely.

Chapter 10: Airplane Disaster

I am a master of timing, sometimes to a fault. But few things make me as happy as watching plans come together. Travel is one of the hardest situations to control from a timing perspective because there are so many elements involved, most of which are out of my control. That makes it all the sweeter when everything goes according to plan. However, there are times, even for me, when the timing goes completely wrong.

I was traveling home after a funeral and had the option to fly instead of making the 15-hour drive. Ideally, I do not like to use the bathroom on the plane, so I carefully plan my beverage intake so I can use the restroom before boarding and wait until after landing to go again.

Because I eat a fairly healthy diet, at roughly the same time every day, my internal processes also run on a schedule. Within thirty minutes, I can usually predict them. On this particular day, however, I was not able to line everything up before my flight.

As the plane took off and we got underway, a certain discontent began to stir in my gut. Nothing serious at first, but as the flight continued, it became obvious that I would not make it through this two-hour trip without a bathroom break.

Not ideal, but manageable if timed well. I waited until the flight attendants were serving passengers and had passed my seat. That way, I would not be in their way, and there would be less traffic to and from the bathroom. So, I got up, walked down the aisle, and made my way inside. So far, so good.

I took care of business, finished the necessary paperwork, and pressed the button to flush. Instead of the expected swoosh and the relief of seeing an empty bowl, the liquid disappeared, but the solid parts stayed behind. Then I heard a faint "ding."

I waited, then pushed the button again. "Ding." No flush.

Panic began to creep in. I washed my hands and tried pouring water from the sink into the toilet, hoping all it needed was a little help. Nope.

Flush. "Ding." Flush. "Ding."

I tried everything I could think of and eventually had to admit defeat. Well. I washed my hands again, straightened myself up, and decided to walk out with my head held high. My plan was simple: leave the scene with dignity and hope no one was waiting outside to discover what I had left behind.

Well, I walked out, and thankfully most people were still seated. My plan to use the bathroom while service was underway had worked, since I was near the back. What I didn't know was that the "ding" I kept hearing was actually ringing throughout the cabin. Apparently, it was some sort of bathroom distress signal.

So, there I was, walking back to my seat with my head held high, doing my best to look inconspicuous, when I noticed the flight attendants talking. About me. They were clearly debating their next move. Should one of them check the bathroom? Should they stop service to deal with what was apparently an emergency?

The moment they saw me, both attendants turned and asked if I was okay. And remember, they had already passed my seat, so this question was asked loudly enough for several rows of passengers to hear.

I had to respond.

"The toilet won't flush."

Mortified. All of my bathroom business had broadcast its failure across the plane with that relentless ding. I had nearly caused the flight attendants to abandon their beverage service and rush in to investigate. And now, as food service wrapped up, the line to the bathroom started forming in earnest. We were one toilet down. Thanks to me.

Then I heard the dreaded "ding" from the other bathroom. Great. No more bathrooms. If I could have blinked myself to another destination or folded into my carry-on, I would have. I couldn't get off that plane fast enough.

Thankfully, through some miracle of modern technology, both bathrooms started working again fairly quickly, and all was well.

Until the flight attendant walked up to me to announce that the bathroom was working again.

Even the best of us have moments when our timing is completely off. In those situations, the only thing to do is wash your hands, walk out with your head held high, and move on. Sometimes, that's all you can do.

LEADERSHIP TOOLBOX

This section can be read straight through or used as a reference. Each chapter begins with a memorable heading and is followed by an explanation of the specific skill it describes. You can read it in sequence to build a broader perspective, or you can jump directly to the chapter that addresses your immediate need. Ideally, return to this section when you're looking to solve a problem, sharpen your approach, or refresh your memory on a particular topic.

TRIANGLE OF PROTECTION: MANAGING AND ACCOUNTABILITY IN A CROSS-CULTURAL WORKPLACE

I begin with this tool because managing people in a cross-cultural environment can be one of the greatest challenges for Black leaders. In fact, holding an employee accountable can sometimes be one of the most professionally risky acts in the workplace. Here is the approach I use.

First, a word of caution: this method will not shield you from discrimination or outright racism. What it does provide, however, is a clear framework to ensure you lead with both grace and a commitment to excellence. It allows you to demonstrate that you've done everything within your power to be fair, consistent, and principled.

This framework, what I call the triangle of protection, rests on three pillars: the law, company policy, and universal application.

Follow the Law

The first part should be obvious: obey the law. But there are times when you might not even realize you're breaking one. Years ago, while serving as a general manager for a national jewelry chain, I was told I would be required to work the last three weeks of December without a single day off. What my boss didn't know, or chose to ignore, was that in Wisconsin, State Statute 103.85 requires employees in factories and retail establishments to have one day off in seven (Wisconsin Legislature: 103.85(1)).

If I had followed those instructions, I would have been violating state law.

Technically, I could have signed a written waiver to forfeit that right, but why would I do that?

Now imagine if I had turned around and demanded the same of my employees. Suppose one of them filed a complaint with the state. Do you think the company would have accepted responsibility, or would they have left me to face the penalties and fines alone?

The lesson is simple: know the law. Use every tool available. Google it. Email your local Department of Labor. Hire a lawyer when you need clarification. In all your getting, get understanding.

Organizational Policies

The next principle is similar: know and follow your organization's policies. This, too, sounds simple, but many people receive their employee handbook, sign off that they've read it, and then toss it aside. I suggest you treat your company's policies the same way you treat an insurance policy. It may be cumbersome to read, but when you need it, it can save your professional life.

I learned this lesson the hard way in my early twenties while working as a security guard at a bank processing center on the border of two small towns in Georgia. My supervisor sent mixed signals about what it meant to be a "good employee." The handbook was clear: no distractions at your post, no radios, phones, or newspapers. But in reality, radios were at each of the three stations, and reading newspapers was common and openly accepted. To top it off, my boss even kept a small TV in her desk.

Then came September 11. In the wake of the terrorist attacks, fear was rampant, and the bank rushed to increase security at the processing center. To be clear, while the tragedy was real and the loss of life incalculable, I don't believe a processing center straddling two small Georgia towns was anywhere near a target list. Still, the company ramped up precautions, offering overtime instead of hiring additional staff. Originally, we had three posts: the parking gate, the front door, and the loading dock. After 9/11, they added two more: one roaming the grounds and another stationed at the delivery gate.

One of the worst parts of working security is that it's nearly impossible to feel like you're doing a "great job." You're expected to stay vigilant, but nothing ever happens. And eight hours of nothing is a lot. A whole lot.

Naturally, I started finding distractions. At first, it was the radio. After a while, I'd heard every song, so I switched stations. Then came talk radio. But even there, the debates eventually blurred together, just the same arguments recycled across different topics. To break up the monotony, I added card games, the newspaper, the occasional phone call. Eventually, I even bought myself a mini-TV like the one my boss kept in her desk. One night I got caught watching it and was told never to do it again. I agreed, knowing the TV was pushing the envelope, but the truth was, I was bored out of my mind.

Fast forward to a night shift where my assignment was simple: record the identification numbers of delivery trucks as they entered the gate. The important detail here is that I didn't control the gate.

The switch that opened it was in the parking lot attendant's booth. My role was just to sit at the delivery post and take down the numbers.

That night, another guard saw a truck approaching and hit the switch to open the gate. The driver, seeing the gate already wide open, assumed it was clear to proceed. He barreled down the short driveway, headed straight for the entrance. Just as he reached it, the automatic timer kicked in. The gate closed right in front of him, and the truck plowed into it. No injuries, thankfully, but the gate was demolished.

The next day, I showed up to work and found the entire place buzzing with one topic: me. Everyone was saying I was going to be written up for the gate incident. First, I was appalled that my supposed "disciplinary issue" was common gossip. Second, I was furious. How could I be blamed for something I had zero control over? I didn't even have access to the gate switch.

When my supervisor finally sat me down, she claimed I could have prevented the accident. According to her, I must have been watching TV in my car, and that is why it happened. I was stunned. Furious. I did not even have the TV with me that night, but how do you prove a negative? All I could do was shake my head as she pinned the blame on me.

Yes, I had seen the accident unfold, but what was I supposed to do? Jump out in front of a speeding UPS truck? Of course not. Yet there I was, accused of negligence, with no real way to defend myself.

And that is when I learned the hard truth: if I had consistently followed company policy to the letter, I would not have left myself vulnerable to such outrageous claims. Deviating, even in ways that seemed harmless or even normal in that work culture, gave people ammunition to use against me later.

Know the policies, and follow them. If a supervisor suggests otherwise, get it in writing. Your employee handbook may not be exciting reading, but when the moment comes, it might just save your career.

<u>Apply Standards "Universally"</u>

The third point in the triangle of protection is to apply your standards to everyone. This ensures you are not discriminating against anyone. Most people believe they are fair and hold everyone to the same standard. Maybe you are that one special person who has somehow managed to avoid unconscious bias and is completely self-aware. For the rest of us, let's explore how we can use this principle to strengthen our leadership journey.

The first step in applying a standard is defining that standard. Let's use a common workplace issue: timeliness. If your employees start their workday at 9 a.m., what does it mean to be "on time"? That might sound obvious, but there are many ways to interpret being "on time" depending on cultural context, past experiences, and other factors.

Do you expect your staff to be at their stations ready to work at 9 a.m.? Does it count if they are in the parking lot by 9 a.m.? What if they arrive at 9 a.m. and are at their desks but still half dressed and eating breakfast? You see the problem. Your standard isn't truly a standard until it's clearly defined.

Once you define it, you must communicate the standard. Repeatedly. Consistently. And you must communicate it verbally, in writing, and through your own behavior. Leaders are often viewed as the ultimate standard. You are paid the most, and you are the most committed to the work. So whatever you do sets the upper limit of what your staff will do as they follow you. If you want people to be on time, and that means ready to work at 9 a.m. at their stations, you had better arrive at 8:45 and be working by 8:59.

The other way your standards need to be communicated is through how you value work, praise staff, promote people, and hold underperformers accountable. A word of caution here: before you set a personal standard, make sure your ideas align with the company's vision and comply with the laws in your area. Confirm that your boss approves of the standard and will support you if a complaint arises. Also, have a plan for when your standard is challenged, because it will be.

I also recommend that your standards consider not only what you need as an employer but also the well-being of your staff. Apply them across the full spectrum of behavior. For example, your standards about timeliness should address both the start and end of the workday. Those standards should mirror each other. If you are strict about requiring people to be at their stations ready to work at 9 a.m., then you should also be strict about ensuring they leave at 5 p.m. If you allow some flexibility at the end of the day, extend that same grace to the start.

Finally, once you have identified and defined your standard, communicated it, and woven it into the culture, keep a written record of how the staff is doing in aligning with it. And do not just document the people who fall short, that is the easiest mistake to make. If you only track the employee who is consistently five to ten minutes late, you will miss acknowledging the employee who consistently arrives early and is ready to work. That person may grow frustrated if they are repeatedly required to stay late to make up for delays caused by others.

Keep a written record of each employee's adherence to the standard. Who is excelling? Acknowledge it. Better yet, celebrate it publicly to add cultural weight to the desired behavior. Then, have quick, focused conversations with each employee about their performance.

"I really appreciate your dedication to showing up on time."

"Your timeliness communicates your professionalism."

Once you get in the habit of recognizing positive behavior, it becomes much easier to address poor performance when it happens. It also helps you remain curious about the reasons behind an employee's behavior instead of immediately assigning blame.

By following this method, if you reach a point where discipline or termination is necessary, you can confidently state that you established the standard in line with company policy and local laws, communicated it clearly, and had multiple conversations with the employee before taking action. If the employee claims they were singled out, you have documentation to counter that false accusation. If they insist they were unaware of the expectation or misunderstood the assignment, you can produce records that demonstrate otherwise.

Emotional Metabolism

This is a concept I developed as an introvert trying to explain my depletion of "people energy" to more extroverted coworkers and friends. I began to wonder if, much like eating food, people "ingest" emotions and need time to process that emotional energy before releasing it.

As it turns out, neuroscientists have been exploring this very idea. Recent research shows that when mammals experience an adverse stimulus, the brain produces two emotional responses. The first is fast and spreads quickly throughout the brain. The second unfolds more slowly and requires time for full processing (Kauvar et al., 2025).

Scientists are still uncovering the exact nature and duration of this second response. For our purposes, two facts matter. First, when you encounter a negative experience as a leader, you will have an immediate emotional reaction. Second, after that initial reaction, you will experience a slower, secondary round of emotional processing that can influence your thinking and behavior.

I call this process, the initial reaction followed by a secondary period of emotional processing, emotional metabolism. Just as with food, we "ingest" emotions and then absorb them into both our bodies and our psyche.

Metabolism itself is defined as "the chemical changes in living cells by which energy is provided for vital processes and activities and new material is assimilated" (Merriam-Webster, 2025). Emotional metabolism, then, becomes a parallel concept. It is the way we transform raw emotional experiences into processed energy that either fuels or drains us.

> I define emotional metabolism as **the emotional and physiological changes in our minds and bodies that provide the fuel for human connection, which shapes the way we see ourselves, others, and the world**.

This framework is important because, as leaders, we rarely think about the need to metabolize our emotional interactions, responses, and desires. To illustrate this concept, I created a typology that describes how I've seen people process emotions and how I've engaged in this activity myself.

Each type identifies a common practice of ingesting emotional material. The next phase describes how that emotional material is processed. I don't believe a person is just one type. Instead, we may experience any of these types, or a combination, during an emotional moment. My goal is not to place people in a box but to help you, as a Black leader, ask yourself three questions as you navigate uncertain times and dangerous systems:

1. How am I processing my emotions in this moment?

2. What do I need to do to metabolize, or make good use of, this emotional incident?

3. How do I get rid of the emotional waste?

Why is this important? Imagine eating breakfast and lunch, drinking a cup of coffee and two bottles of water, but never taking a bathroom break while at work. How productive would you be in that state? How much of a mess would you create when you just couldn't hold it all in any longer?

Now imagine that right after lunch, someone asks you to attend another lunch meeting. Would you be able to eat more? Should you? Would your lack of eating damage the relationship? If you did eat, would you be fully present for the meeting, or too distracted by your physical discomfort to engage with the discussion?

You get the point. Far too often, as Black leaders, we keep pushing through work and life without considering our emotional health in a way that honors both the need for resilience and the need for rest. Older generations often ignored mental health, while younger generations sometimes focus on it so intently that they risk losing resilience. Either way, we need a new model. I will describe the three types below, and then I'll leave you with a challenge.

The Grazer

This emotional metabolic type focuses on one kind of interaction and then ruminates on it repeatedly. Processing is ongoing.

Positive Emotional Example: A person believes they look good and that others respect them. They are very aware of the looks they receive, interpreting ambiguous glances as admiration and negative expressions as jealousy rather than signs that something is wrong with their outfit or personality. They collect these interactions and reflect on them throughout the day, which adds to their sense of self-worth and self-esteem.

Negative Emotional Example: A person who feels self-conscious about their appearance and struggles with self-confidence interprets the looks they receive differently. They assume anyone who glances at them is judging their flaws. Smiles become precursors to jokes at their expense, and lingering looks are taken as signs of disgust or derision. They collect these interactions throughout the day, each one chipping away at their self-esteem as they revisit and re-examine them.

The Constrictor

This emotional metabolic type does not ingest often, but when it does, it swallows the whole experience at once. Digestion is slow and requires significant effort. This type cannot move forward until digestion is complete or nearly so.

Positive Emotional Example: A person is surprised by a loved one with an expensive gift or an act of service. They are thankful and appreciative, expressing their gratitude immediately. Yet as they sit with the moment, and for days afterward, they continue to process the impact of the gesture. They realize they needed that infusion of love more than they had recognized. The following day, they explain how meaningful it was to be honored by someone so busy. Soon after, they feel guilty about being the center of attention and resolve those feelings by deciding to do something kind in return. They sit with these emotions for a week or more before returning to normal.

Negative Emotional Example: A person is called a racial slur in a meeting, and the matter is dismissed as the meeting ends. Shocked and hurt, they do not know how to respond in the moment. They return to work but cannot concentrate. An hour later, they decide to take the rest of the day off. On the drive home, anger surfaces, and they replay the meeting in their mind, cursing the offender. At home, they are overcome with sadness. Later, they feel ashamed that they did not respond in the meeting. The next day, their anger shifts to frustration with colleagues who stayed silent in the moment but offered quiet support at the water cooler. After a few days of processing and seeking advice, they decide to report the incident. Soon after, they realize reporting is not enough and determine they must address the offender personally. They sit with these emotions until that conversation takes place and may not feel normal again for two weeks or more.

The Hunter

This emotional metabolic type is characterized by a person recognizing they need a particular kind of interaction or affirmation and then actively seeking out the desired stimulus. They are selective in what they ingest but relentless in their pursuit.

Positive Emotional Example: A person wants friends and family to spend time with them and show love through quality connection. To meet this need, they decide to host a birthday trip where everyone is free from distractions and can focus fully on one another instead of outside obligations. They plan the trip in detail, persuade others to join, and keep up with the arrangements to ensure the event succeeds. As the celebration unfolds, they document and share the experience, creating a story they can use to encourage even reluctant friends or family to join next time.

Negative Emotional Example: A person avoids acknowledging their own feelings of inadequacy and instead seeks relationships that give them power over others. They are drawn to people in need of help or caught in distress, stepping in to provide stability and support. Once an emotional connection forms, they feel an irresistible pull toward the person, and a relationship begins. Problems emerge when their partner grows tired of being the weaker link and either leaves or demands greater balance. The relationship may collapse, leaving the person feeling used or betrayed. In time, they begin searching for another vulnerable individual, repeating the cycle again.

This leadership tool is not about perfectly identifying your typology. Instead, it is about gaining clarity on the way you receive and process emotional information and stimuli. Once you understand your own internal process, the next step is to pay attention to how those you lead and work alongside metabolize their emotions as well.

If you are planning a long meeting, do you build in emotional breaks? Should you introduce a new concept in one meeting and then reconvene a week later, allowing people the time they need to process before moving forward? How do you prepare to handle emotional outbursts from an employee with wisdom and composure?

This tool is still a work in progress. As scientific research advances, I will continue to refine and strengthen it. But even in its early form, I believe you can already see how powerful emotional metabolism can be for managing yourself and leading others effectively.

Once you gain insight into your emotional metabolism, you will also need practical questions that help you navigate the sea of feelings and interpersonal relationships. That is where the next tool comes in: the F-it Method.

F-It: Emotional Regulation for the Busy Leader

As a Black leader, there is one thing I can guarantee: people will work your last nerve at some point or another. What's also true is that most of leadership is about people working together to achieve a goal. Communication is difficult and full of potential pitfalls. The challenges go on and on. As a leader, how are you supposed to navigate all of these obstacles while maintaining your dignity, composure, and your job?

Let me introduce you to my favorite mnemonic device, one that helps me remember how to keep myself grounded in tense emotional situations while still maintaining my dignity:

F-it!

No, it's not what it appears to be at first. The method comprises three elements:

Feelings, Facts, and Forward.

These are three questions you can ask yourself to process emotions and determine the best method of response.

<u>Feelings</u>

This is the first step. How do you feel about what happened? How do you feel about what was said, or what wasn't said? It's important to resist the temptation to censor or diminish what you're feeling in the moment. It's okay to experience one feeling now and a different one later. If you haven't read the section on Emotional Metabolism, stop and read that first, then come back and finish this section.

I don't know how you were raised or what sort of work environment you operate in, but I do know it can be tough to be Black, emotional, and expressive in the workplace. Your tone might be construed as violence, or your vocal disagreement might label you a loner, someone incapable of being a team player. If you're a Black woman, you might exist in a space where even professional expression of your feelings is scrutinized. If you're a Black man, perhaps you've been taught that expressing any emotion beyond joy or anger isn't manly.

All that can lead us to a place where we don't acknowledge or sit with our own emotions. So, the first question you must ask yourself is, **"What am I feeling?"**

Here's an example. At the time of writing, I have recently been appointed as the new president of a local non-profit, Nehemiah, replacing our founder and long-time president, Dr. Gee. The transition was beautiful, and he is now the Board Chair and President Emeritus. He recruited me, trained me, and eventually turned over leadership to me. The day after the transition became official, I felt strange. I was having a hard time celebrating and receiving the praise people lavished on me. It didn't seem right, so I asked myself that question:

"What am I feeling?"

It turned out that I was feeling guilty because I believed I had "taken" Dr. Gee's identity as president. Now, that framing isn't correct. He nominated me for the position. His transition wasn't connected to any failure or scandal. He had started another non-profit and had successfully led Nehemiah for 35 years, including two years of planning and 33 years once Nehemiah launched. I didn't take anything from him. It was a transformation for both of us. Once I realized that, Dr. Gee and I had an impromptu discussion about our respective feelings. Both of us were experiencing some surprising emotions, but neither of us regretted the decision.

That conversation and my processing led me to understand that part of what I had accepted when I took the role of president wasn't just a job, but a new identity. I could no longer attend events as Harry H. Hawkins III. I was now attending events as Harry, President of Nehemiah. My presence, or lack thereof, communicated something about the values of the organization. To be successful, I had to adopt this new identity.

This was tricky for me because I grew up on the mean streets of retail sales. In retail, I learned that promotions and demotions came so swiftly and regularly that I had better not attach my persona to a position, because it could be taken away on a whim.

So, part of my hesitation to engage was due to a fear I had "learned" while working in retail. I had to let that go in order to move forward.

Facts

If you were paying attention to the previous story, you noticed the second "F," Facts. Now that you've examined your feelings, we need to ask the second question: What are the facts associated with the feelings? In my example, Dr. Gee nominated me for the position. The Board unanimously approved my appointment. I didn't have the organizational power to "take" anything from Dr. Gee.

These facts helped me frame my emotions and compare them to reality. This second step is not about changing your emotions. Rather, your task here is to understand how much your feelings are aligned with the facts. The way they are aligned is not nearly as important as recognizing that there is a relationship between the two. What I mean is that while I can acknowledge that I could not, in fact, take anything from my boss, it is still okay to recognize that I felt that way.

This step is simple, but it is also the one most often overlooked when people are responding to their emotions. Don't skip this step, because if you do, you risk making decisions based solely on your emotions. That can lead you to abandon the triangle of protection and fail to extend the same standard to everyone.

Forward

Now that you've processed your emotions and highlighted the facts surrounding the moment, it's time for our third question: **How do you move forward?**

In my example, I needed to become comfortable with my new role so I could fulfill the responsibilities that came along with it. Attending community events, evening gatherings, and personal celebrations suddenly became part of what it meant to do a good job.

For me, this question is really asking: What is your goal? What do you want to happen after this moment is over? How are you going to exist in the space or in the relationship once this moment has passed?

There's not much more to it than that. My assumption is that as a leader, once you are confronted with your emotions and the facts, you will have enough knowledge and skill in your area of expertise to see a path forward.

Professional and Personal Standard

This is a tool that I've hinted at in a few sections, but now it is time to explore the idea in greater detail.

All the previous tools in the leadership toolbox, once combined, will make up the framework for your standard as a leader. This topic is worthy of its own book and deep reflective study. However, I will ask you a few questions that will help you create your own standard.

First, let's define a standard. Webster's defines *standard* as "something established by authority, custom, or general consent as a model or example" (Definition of STANDARD, 2025). A professional standard, then, is a set of guiding principles that serve as a model for a leader's behavior and interpersonal interactions.

To tackle this extraordinarily complex topic, I will break it down into three elements: identity, persona, and organizational role. I will define each one, explain how to master the relevant element, and then we will begin constructing a mock set of standards.

Identity

The dictionary defines *identity* as "the distinguishing character or personality of an individual" (Definition of IDENTITY, 2025). Who you are as a person is the foundation of your personal and professional standard. Everything you do flows out of this reality, serving as a framework for understanding yourself and the world, and as a means of connecting with others. There are entire sections of books and countless studies that attempt to quantify and articulate the best way to understand oneself.

If you are a busy Black leader, I will make two assumptions about you. The first is that you don't have a lot of time to go on a self-discovery journey to explore every corner of your personality. The second is that you already have some level of self-awareness when it comes to who you are.

With that in mind, I suggest a particular method to articulate the major parts of your personality, or at least enough traits to begin constructing your set of boundaries. Write down descriptive sentences. If you can, use adjectives to describe yourself.

For example: I am a loyal friend. I am time-conscious. If that feels difficult, don't worry. Whatever you write will work. The adjectives simply make the next step easier.

Here are three ways I would describe myself as an individual:

I am time-conscious.

I am a problem solver.

I am a family man.

Take time to write down your list. Don't attempt to do this in your head. There is something powerful in writing down your identity markers. Once you have a few items, you can stop. I suggest at least three. If you create a longer list, select the top five that mean the most to you.

Now that you have completed the exercise, let me explain how to master the art of identity: self-awareness. How was the exercise? Did you find it easy to write down elements of your personality? Did you struggle to articulate who you are in a few sentences? Did you have to hold yourself back from writing too much?

Whatever your answer, the key to mastering this foundational principle is the ability to understand yourself. Why do you think the way you do? What shaped, and continues to shape, your view of the world? How does your personality influence the way you relate to others?

The trick here is to realize that this understanding, this self-awareness, is a continuous journey. Even if you understood yourself at one stage of life, people change as they age and as they take on new roles in their personal and professional lives. Relationships can influence how we see ourselves and how we define who we are. Education, experience, and countless other encounters shape us as well. So do not be afraid to treat this exercise and the resulting boundary as a working draft. If you need help understanding yourself, re-read the F-it section and follow the instructions there.

Another challenge might be that you are focused on your flaws. That is okay, but I encourage you to rewrite those problems as positive traits. Change "I'm always late" to "I have a flexible relationship with time." That shift allows you to acknowledge that your strength can be a problem in some situations, but it can also be an asset in the right circumstances. Being late for work is a problem, but the ability to pivot in the moment is a jewel when emergencies arise.

Persona

The next element we need to deal with is persona. The dictionary defines *persona* as "an individual's social façade" (Definition of PER-SONA, 2025). I like to think of your persona as both the façade you wear in public and the role society expects you to play in the larger community.

Let me shape your expectations from the beginning. Your persona and your identity will never be fully aligned. Why do I say that? Because to exist in a society, we all make concessions as social creatures in order to remain in relationship with others. This is even more true for Black leaders, women, or members of other minority groups. The key is to understand what your persona is and to create as much alignment with your identity as possible.

Here's an example. Let's say you identify as someone who refuses to be disrespected. If someone is rude to you, your true self might want to curse them out and slap them in the face. But you adopt a persona that restrains that response because you do not want to deal with the consequences, whether physical or legal. Instead, your persona, the personality you adopt, responds by speaking up to highlight the disrespect. While that may not be your "true" self, it is a concession based on the reality of your personality.

Think of your persona as the connectors that link you to the other people in your world. Then, make a list similar to the previous one. Who are you in public?

I am polite.

I am a hard worker.

I am impatient with disorder.

Take the time to write down your list. Once you have it, examine the places where your identity and your persona clash. Are there tensions between these two worlds? Sometimes tensions exist simply because of the nature of the relationship. Take parenting, for example. If a child acts in a way that an adult did, you might respond much more harshly. Yet as a parent, you might adopt the persona of being understanding in that heated moment to help the child navigate through the challenge.

Those types of tensions are normal. What I am more interested in are the tensions that are ongoing.

In navigating these tensions, we begin to see the first pillars of your standard emerge. How do you know when someone has pushed you too far? How do you know when you have given enough?

The concept of a boundary often brings to mind lines and borders. Instead, imagine overlapping circles forming a Venn diagram. You have gone too far when you are no longer your true self, or when your persona no longer relates to your identity in any meaningful way.

Let's explore a few examples using my own list. I identified myself as a problem solver. At work, my persona is one that works hard. Usually, there is no conflict between these two elements. However, there are times when these realities can clash. Imagine a situation where my hard work is taken advantage of, and I keep inheriting tasks from a co-worker who is constantly behind. I see the problem: the co-worker is not being held accountable. Yet I lack the authority to correct the situation.

In that case, I can go to my supervisor and express my concerns. If that does not resolve the issue, the tension grows, leaving me with an internal conflict. Who am I, really? Does my identity as a family man require that I keep my job, which means viewing the situation through the lens of maintaining employment? Or do I lean into my identity as a problem solver, continuing to suggest solutions and address the problem until it is either fixed or I am fired?

In each case, there is a constant negotiation we go through as we live in relationship and proximity with others. Building on our definition of a standard, I suggest that to begin constructing a set of personal and professional standards, you must agree within yourself on how you will handle certain repeated negotiations.

When my identity as a family man is threatened by my hard-worker persona in the case of working overtime, how do I decide whether to work?

When I am faced with the dilemma of solving a problem but the path forward might require impolite conversations, how do I handle that?

If you are an introspective person, you can think through these and other possible scenarios to articulate and define your standard. However, do not spend all of your time trying to determine the right or perfect way to respond. You will not be able to anticipate every scenario, nor predict how you will feel or react when a particular set of circumstances arises. Your standard is a guide, not an unbreakable law.

If you are not a very introspective person, then try to understand why you responded the way you did. You might even ask those who know you well and care about you to help you talk through your usual responses. In fact, others may recognize your patterns more readily and more deeply than you can on your own.

Organizational Role

There is one other element we need to incorporate into your standard creation: your organizational role. Your position at work or in any organization can impact how you apply and contextualize your other identities. The challenge of working extra hours looks very different if you are a salesperson compared to a store manager. You may be able to refuse to work longer hours if you work for someone else, but if you are the business owner, your options may be limited in certain circumstances.

Let me share a story that illustrates how I used my own standard in a previous job. I was the general manager at a jewelry store, where, when fully staffed, we had four managers including myself. At that time, however, we were missing one manager.

The organization offered its leaders a great tool in digital form that allowed us to create action plans for employee improvement. I found the best way to use this tool was through biweekly check-ins. In these meetings, we would address the issue, problem-solve the root cause, and lay out a plan for improvement.

Typically, my recommended cadence meant an employee would work an average of six shifts between reviews, not including weekends. Weekends were extremely busy, and people often fell back into old habits during times of stress. The process worked well across the organization. At some point, however, one of the executives decided that if a little worked well, then a lot would be better. Leadership mandated that every store conduct eight of these reviews each week.

Without boring you with the math, that idea did not work for my store for two reasons. First, we were missing a manager. Second, and even more important, we did not have enough sales staff to complete both the required number of reviews and maintain the two-week cadence. As a result, some staff would have only two or three shifts to make a change before we spoke again. Three shifts were not enough to see any real improvement.

My store was able to reliably complete five or six reviews each week. I would log in to the system, plan for eight, and simply delete the reviews we didn't get to. I thought it was a good compromise, since my bosses could see we were attempting to comply, even though we never managed to hit the stated goal.

One day my supervisor called to discuss our progress. I explained all the reasons why it was unreasonable to expect us to comply with the request. She told me we needed to plan for all eight, and if we scheduled a review, we had to submit it instead of deleting it.

This is where my identity as a problem solver and my persona as a hard worker clashed. I could not work any harder at completing the task. The math made it impossible. We did not have enough staff to sustain the cadence that produced meaningful results. On the other hand, if I followed the directive exactly as prescribed, and I did a few times, the employees did not make progress, and my credibility as a leader suffered. The process, which was designed to align employees and leadership in support of growth, became instead a tool for criticism and disciplinary action.

I raised my concerns in meetings and with peers. The advice I got was simply to complete the reviews. To me, it made no sense to waste time filling out paperwork that did not help employees improve and instead damaged morale. I could not comply with actually doing the reviews. Some people even suggested that I just fill in the fields and pretend the review had been done, even if it hadn't. I assumed others were doing this, since I was the only one who got in trouble for not following instructions.

Beyond the dishonesty, the issue I had with that approach was that the reviews became part of the employee's official file. To anyone looking at the record, it would appear that the employee had been trained multiple times in an area where they were not improving. If another manager came along later, they might assume the person was beyond help, when in fact they had never received meaningful coaching.

So, I did what I could to align my identity and my persona with my organizational role. I planned all eight reviews. I submitted the five or six we actually completed. For the rest, I filled in each field with a number. If anyone looked closely, it would be clear that the employee had not actually worked on the topics listed in the form.

Of course, this did not go well. When I was confronted about my "fluff" forms, I explained exactly why I had done it and refused to back down from my stance. I was not going to compromise my integrity as a person or my drive to solve problems. Soon after, I was demoted.

There is both power and danger in having and holding to a standard. It can, and probably will, cost you something along the way: opportunity, jobs, relationships, or money. However, I have found that whatever the issue, it is better for me to face challenges with my sense of self intact than to allow others to define the boundaries of my identity.

If you have never tried to articulate your standard, don't attempt to write an entire personal manifesto. Start by highlighting the areas that are easiest to define, or explore the areas where you are experiencing the most conflict. Start small, build often, and don't be afraid to adjust as you learn more about yourself, others, and your growth in leadership and in life.

Culture of Curiosity

M y personality, according to my Myers-Briggs results (INTJ), is one full of judgment. That means I am comfortable with closed-ended ideas. I don't like open-ended thoughts or unfinished business. In relationships, that often means I am almost always sure about what something is, what was meant, or whether it was good or bad.

I spend a lot of time gathering data, researching, and observing people and systems before making judgments, so I am often right, not because I know it all, but because I have studied for decades.

However, that is rarely true when it comes to understanding other people's motivations or emotions. That is why this leadership tool is so important. It allows me to work with others and maintain good relationships. I have to intentionally slow down and ask myself if I really know what I think I know.

The process I use is the F-it method I described earlier. If you skipped that section, go back and read it before continuing here. As a leader, it is not enough to have a process for regulating your emotions;

you also have to help your team or staff do the same. Let me illustrate this with a story.

My first real leadership role in an organization came when I was 17 and was voted in as the band captain of the Chamblee High School marching band. I had risen through the ranks of both musical and organizational leadership, and I thought I knew exactly what my job would be as captain: helping people memorize music, learn drill, and perfect our routine before we went to festival.

Throughout the entire season, I had only one conversation about music. The rest of my time was spent talking with people about their emotions. To be clear, if you haven't picked up on this yet, I hated talking about emotions. At that age, I didn't even want to discuss my own, much less wrestle with someone else's. My comfort lies in systems thinking, which is why I have created so many systems to help engage with emotions.

But I learned a valuable lesson that year. People management is mostly about managing people and their relationships with each other. To do that well, you have to help others, at least in the workplace, regulate their emotions.

Now, as a leader, I often wish people had learned how to regulate their emotions before they came to work for me. You might be tempted to belittle someone who struggles with this as an adult, but I have found that the problem is not a lack of childhood lessons. Instead, it is the reality of navigating a complicated and ever-changing system of self-awareness combined with the willingness to engage in uncomfortable transformation work.

Why is that? When you are four years old and cranky, you can take a nap. But when you are forty and exhausted, a nap in the middle of the day is a luxury few can afford. So even if you learned this skill at an early age, as you grow, your responsibilities change, your body shifts, and your relationships evolve. The tactics you use to regulate emotions must change with life.

As a leader, you must help your team navigate this minefield of emotions and interpretations. I divide that work into two approaches: one proactive and the other reactive.

Proactive

This is simple, and it can even be fun. People often enjoy exploring differences with each other outside of conflicts. Think of lighthearted icebreaker activities: What song best describes you when you wake up in the morning? What is a must-have at Thanksgiving dinner? Whatever fits your culture and team, find ways to highlight that everyone thinks, feels, and experiences life differently than their co-workers.

Scenarios are another way to expose these differences. For example: If such-and-such happened, what would you do first, and why?

You get the point. You already know that people are different and will react to events and interactions based on their uniqueness. The key is to explore that before it becomes a problem.

How can you do that? Here are some of the ways I have tackled this need in the past.

I have used personality tests, such as the Myers-Briggs or Strengths Finder, to quickly and openly explore the motivations and traits of my staff. There are many tools available, and while none provide a complete picture of a person, each offers a valuable window into how someone operates.

Another method I have found useful is to discuss differences in a way that allows those differences to breathe. Food is my go-to option here. Most people will accept that someone does not like a certain dish, but often only because we believe they have not had the "right" version yet. I have found food to be an easy way to discuss preferences, diet choices, religious beliefs, family practices, and culture in a way that feels inclusive and relatively safe. And when disagreements about the "best" dish arise, they can be settled with a cook-off or bake-off, productive and delicious!

Your approach will depend on the culture and practices of your organization. How much time do you have to spend getting to know one another better? Does your whole staff gather on a regular basis? Do you work in an environment where people are more technical and less engaged with emotions? Do you work in a highly regulated environment that demands precise time management to meet production quotas?

Whatever your situation, you will need to contextualize the concept in order to apply it effectively to your workplace or group.

<u>Reactive</u>

This approach works best when navigating problems between employees or group members. I like to listen first, then ask questions. What happened? Why did they do that?

The key to this approach is not dismissing the issues, but instead guiding the employee or group member to be empathetic. Can they understand why someone acted or reacted the way they did?

The goal here is simple: help people place the impact of someone's actions into one bucket and fill the bucket of intentions with lots of questions. Once both are explored, the solution to the problem can be sought and implemented.

This section is simple, but do not confuse simple with easy. There are no shortcuts to implementing this concept. It will take all of your leadership skills to do it well. It will take time, probably more time than you want to devote to it. But rest assured, this is where you will spend most of your time as a leader: developing a team that can navigate personal differences and the difficulties of working with other people.

PUSH OR PULL?

This concept is not of my own making, but I will include a brief description here along with a reference for where you can learn more.

In the book *Leading Across Boundaries*, Linden (2010) writes, "Push is direct, sometimes forceful, using the power of authority" (p. 84). He goes on to explain that "Pull taps an inner need or motivation, it connects with something that the person already wants to do" (p. 85).

In a recent Justified Anger Leadership Institute session, I introduced this concept to the leaders in that cohort, and they immediately saw the benefits of applying it to their leadership style and approach.

If you want to read more about the concept of push and pull, I recommend reading that section of Linden's book. It is well worth the price of the book just for that one idea.

What I will discuss here in more detail is how to apply this concept as a Black leader. For me, push, relying on my authority to enforce behavior, worked best when policies, laws, or ethical concerns were at play.

For example, when I worked at a jewelry store, we were required for safety reasons to enter the building at the same time each morning. If someone was late, that became a safety issue, and I would use my authority to enforce compliance with the company's time guidelines. Everyone knew that if you were scheduled to open, you had to be exiting your vehicle at 8:57 for a 9:00 a.m. shift. It took three minutes to enter the building, disarm the alarm system, and clock in.

No compassion was extended to those who struggled with punctuality. If you missed the 8:57 window, you could expect to wait until 10:00 a.m. when the store opened.

On the other hand, I would use pull when I wanted someone to address a performance issue. I needed to tap into their personal motivation in order to get them to take the actions I required.

As an example, if a salesperson wanted to earn more money, I would use that desire as a driver to encourage them to offer credit cards more often. Or, if a salesperson wanted a promotion, I would use that ambition to help them think through how they needed to comply with specific areas of improvement.

Again, this is a simple concept but mastering it will take time and effort. The best advice I can offer is to be intentional about the method you are employing. Understand when to apply organizational authority and when to tap into personal motivation. Mastering this concept can make you a better leader almost overnight.

RECOMMENDED READING

<u>Employee Management and Employee Engagement</u>

Carrots and Sticks Don't Work

Love 'Em or Lose 'Em

Leading Across Boundaries

<u>Personal Transformation</u>

The Person Called You

Tyranny of the Urgent

Dream With Me

Black Faces in White Places

How to Change

<u>Social Justice and Social Change</u>

The New Jim Crow

The Heart of Racial Justice

The Roadmap to Reconciliation

Half the Sky

Street Saints

I'm Still Here

History

An Indigenous Peoples' History of the United States

An African American and Latinx History of the United States

The History of White People

Dark Work

Economics and Poverty

When Helping Hurts: How to Alleviate Poverty...

Blood and Money

Accounting for Slavery

Poverty By America

Slavery's Capitalism

Innovation

Surfing the Edge of Chaos

The Art of Innovation

Ten Rules for Strategic Innovators

Innovation Theology

REFERENCES

Aubrey, A. (2024, March 20). U.S. drops in new global happiness ranking. One age group bucks the trend. *NPR*. https://www.npr.org/sections/health-shots/2024/03/20/1239537074/u-s-drops-in-new-global-happiness-ranking-one-age-group-bucks-the-trend

Definition of CULTURE. (2025, August 11). https://www.merriam-webster.com/dictionary/culture

Definition of IDENTITY. (2025, July 6). https://www.merriam-webster.com/dictionary/identity

Definition of METABOLISM. (2025, June 4). https://www.merriam-webster.com/dictionary/metabolism

Definition of PERSONA. (2025, July 5). https://www.merriam-webster.com/dictionary/persona

Definition of STANDARD. (2025, June 22). https://www.merriam-webster.com/dictionary/standard

Hunter, J. D. (2010). *To change the world: The irony, tragedy, and possibility of Christianity in the late modern world.* Oxford University Press.

Kauvar, I., Richman, E. B., Liu, T. X., Li, C., Vesuna, S., Chibukhchyan, A., Yamada, L., Fogarty, A., Solomon, E., Choi, E. Y., Mortazavi, L., Chau Loo Kung, G., Mukunda, P., Raja, C., Gil-Hernández, D., Patron, K., Zhang, X., Brawer, J., Wrobel, S., ... Deisseroth, K. (2025). Conserved brain-wide emergence of emotional response from sensory experience in humans and mice. *Science*, *388*(6750), eadt3971. https://doi.org/10.1126/science.adt3971

Kelley, T. (2001). *The Art of Innovation*. Doubleday.

Kruse, K. (2012, June 22). *What Is Employee Engagement*. Forbes. https://www.forbes.com/sites/kevinkruse/2012/06/22/employee-engagement-what-and-why/

Linden, R. (2010). *Leading Across Boundaries: Creating Collaborative Agencies in a Networked World* (first edition). Jossey-Bass.

Marciano, P. (2010). *Carrots and Sticks Don't Work: Build a Culture of Employee Engagement with the Principles of RESPECT*. McGraw-Hill Companies, Inc.

Merriam-Webster.com Dictionary. (n.d.). *Definition of LEAVEN*. Retrieved February 5, 2025, from https://www.merriam-webster.com/dictionary/leaven

Merriam-Webster.com Dictionary. (2025a, January 29). *Definition of LEVITY*. https://www.merriam-webster.com/dictionary/levity

Merriam-Webster.com Dictionary. (2025b, February 12). *Definition of RECKON*. https://www.merriam-webster.com/dictionary/reckon

Miller, J. (2020, May 11). *The science behind yeast and how to make your own*. Livescience.Com. https://www.livescience.com/yeast-science-how-to-make.html

News, N. (2025, May 29). Emotions Echo: Brainwide Timing Patterns Reveal Roots of Feeling. *Neuroscience News*. https://neurosciencenews.com/emotions-neuroscience-29160/

Pascale, R., Millemann, M., & Gioja, L. (2000). *Surfing the Edge of Chaos: The Laws of Nature and the New Laws of Business*. Three Rivers Press.

Vincent, L. (2017). *Innovation Theology*. Wipf and Stock.